ENTER IN

PREPARATION OF THE HEART FOR AN AUDIENCE WITH A HOLY GOD

Barb Garner

Barb Garner
Ps 27:1

CROSS
BOOKS

CrossBooks™
1663 Liberty Drive
Bloomington, IN 47403
www.crossbooks.com
Phone: 1-866-879-0502

First published by CrossBooks 11/10/2009

ISBN: 978-1-6150-7058-9 (sc)

Library of Congress Control Number: 2009936945

Printed in the United States of America
Bloomington, Indiana

This book is printed on acid-free paper.

TABLE OF CONTENTS

ONCE UPON A TIME . . .

A TALE OF GLORIA, PURE HEART, AND THE KING

Once upon a time there was a lady-in-waiting. Gloria, a daughter of royalty, expectantly waited, with her court, for Pure Heart, a king's son who had chosen her to be his bride. She was fair, her skin soft and creamy. Graceful in movement, she became a subtle presence in a room, and coming from royal lineage, she was rich by the world's standards lacking nothing. A heavenly fragrance filled the room when she entered, lingered long after she left and revealed her royalty. Clothed in rich embroidery and garments of gold, Gloria seemed to be a gorgeous shimmer as you gazed upon her. Beautiful and joyful in the preparation of her outward beauty, yet she questioned whether she could be inwardly worthy enough to belong to Pure Heart.

Requirements for those aspiring to stand in Pure Heart's secret place were decreed by law. One must be utterly innocent in heart, mind, thought, purpose and deed. Their soul was required to be complete in faithfulness and loyalty, and their mind must never be set on vanity, falsehood or impurity. Those with this aspiration must never have sworn deceitfully against another.

What was Gloria to do? Who could say they had made their heart clean? Her thoughts raced to justify her lack of inner beauty. "I am only human, and my way seems right, but I fear for Pure Heart to look on my heart" she moaned. Being aware that the ways of mankind were perverse and strange, she finally accepted the reality that, according to the law her heart was deceitful. In desperation, she cried out "I need help! What can I do to have a clean heart?"

Having chosen Gloria with her inadequacies, Pure Heart stayed nearby and overheard her cry. Without hesitation he answered, "Give me your heart and watch what I will do."

Realizing she could never be good enough to gain acceptance by the King, she chose to accept the sacrificial offer and gave him her heart. The transaction was instantly made. Pure Heart took her imperfection upon himself, out of pure love, removing her from the curse of the law by becoming cursed in her place! Amazingly, the pure and Holy King allowed his only son to become unclean for her. Agonizing moments passed as she witnessed the King's wrath on her impurity being poured out on Pure Heart.

Unaccustomed to being loved that much, Gloria slowly raised her eyes to see Pure Heart standing before her. He held out his arms of love, offering her a new heart, a never-ending life of love and complete acceptance with the King!

Gloria now belonged to Pure Heart! Desiring to know him more, she began following him trusting him for all her needs. He desired her companionship and they spent rich time together. However, these times became more elusive and cumbersome as life in the kingdom slipped into a routine. The demands of purity became tiresome and at times, she no longer felt like royalty. Knowing Pure Heart was always there made their relationship casual and, very slowly, Gloria began to think she did not need special time alone with Pure Heart. Feelings would arise that she could even handle her life using her own strength and perspective. Forgetting that since she had joined her life with Pure Heart, and his desire was to show her how to release his perfect heart and fragrant life through hers, life became dull and colorless. Work once enjoyed now became tiresome and futile. Something was wrong!

One day, Gloria found a drawing of an old tabernacle -a tent used by the King's people who once wandered in the wilderness. The King had provided a blueprint, giving his people specific instructions concerning the proper place and manner in which to approach Him for guidance and strength during their journey to a promised land. As she gazed on the ancient drawings, her heart stirred with a strange new awareness. The King himself had provided a way for the people to meet with him. Her thoughts turned toward Pure Heart and how he was the clearest representation of the King. Could there be a connection between his mighty redemptive act on her behalf and her ability to enter into the King's presence? Could this possibly be an answer for the disappointing routine her life had become? How could she realize her lover's purity and purpose within her own heart? Perhaps the objects and their placement in the tabernacle would offer a way to unlock the mysteries and questions in her heart and help her learn to live a more meaningful life. With every step, Gloria felt closer to Pure Heart. He was calling her to an encounter with his father, the King.

A letter rested near the drawing. Gloria eagerly began to read. Outlined there were instructions about approaching the King. Before entering the tabernacle, preparation was made for the Holy meeting. No one dared rush past the places of self-preparation required by the King. Out of respect, yet drawn by His love, one would follow the steps unlocking the mystery of approaching the King, and Pure Heart was there escorting her into the King's presence. Pausing by each object and place in the tabernacle, Pure Heart would explain its purpose, encouraging her to apply her heart to it's demand.

First, one must quiet the heart. Prayer was to be used in the mind and heart to set aside the physical dimension, becoming aware of an entrance into the spiritual. So many things distracted her heart from this special time with the King. The letter said that the King is a Spirit, and they that encounter Him must encounter Him in spirit and in truth.

5

Gloria spent some time here releasing the distractions of her life and embracing the spiritual nature of her quest.

The altar of sacrifice was next, where an offering was to be presented to Pure Heart. He explained that he could only take what was freely given to him, since it was her personal offering in response to the King's purity. Once given into his hands, he would carry it to the altar and make the sacrifice by fire. Surrendering any impurity in the heart is required before an audience with the King. Pure items will survive the fire, and can be used by the King. Those things consumed by fire give freedom to meet the king unhindered. After all, he cannot allow anything impure to enter his presence.

Pure Heart suggested things in Gloria's heart that would not be allowed. The list included fear, because it displaces faith, a requirement to please the King. Another impurity was distraction, including events, persons, or items which demand and divert our attention and energy away from the King. Following distractions were heart burdening things, such as conflict and grief, since those things keep our focus on ourselves. Finally, perplexing issues having no answers, which would keep the mind pre-occupied, would not be allowed since one would be unable to focus on the instructions from the King.

Gloria knelt before Pure Heart and gave him every impure thing as he made her aware of it. Her heart felt light.

Beyond the altar of sacrifice stood a large brass laver, where Pure Heart washed away the residual stains from her experience at the altar of sacrifice. Each impurity in the heart, once exposed, was confessed as dark and unacceptable and then cleansed as if it never existed. Gloria rose with help from Pure Heart and relished the cleanliness.

Nearby was a curtain leading into a very dark room. Illumined only by a golden candlestick with seven elaborate bowls of light, this was the place of humility. The understanding gained during this time

Gloria knew to be a gift of knowledge and wisdom which could only come from the King, not from her own understanding. If his spirit did not illuminate her heart and mind, there would never be any wisdom or understanding. Pure Heart knew that one could spend a lifetime studying the letter and blueprint never really knowing the author nor the applications for their lives. The King's very spirit would make the letter come alive with understanding for those who spent time with him.

Gazing across the candlelit room, she now viewed a table piled high with loaves of bread. This was the place of thankfulness. The daily presence of fresh loaves of bread was a symbol that the King provided everything needed to live her life. This bread was actually Pure Heart, and was broken through his earlier sacrificial act of love on her behalf, so she might partake of this life of royalty. His life was to be her life - her "daily bread."

Gloria turned to see another curtain, separating the darkened room from another place – the Holy of Holies. Just outside the curtain was another small altar. It was where pure incense burned, becoming an offering of praise sacrificed to the King for his great qualities. Pure adoration, offered with fear and awe was allowing her to anticipate her immediate audience with her King.

As Gloria entered the place called the Holy of Holies, she knew that this was where she would talk with the King. The letter spoke of an earlier time when one special priest was appointed to enter this place to meet with the King once a year. Pure Heart assured her that she now had unlimited access and time with the King because of the price he had paid with his own suffering on her behalf. This place where the King's wisdom, strength, purity, and purpose was to be infused into her heart was a very special place – surely a Holy of Holies. Listening to the King's gentle, loving voice, a "Yes" formed on her lips as she was filled with His love, power, and instructions.

Gloria rose from her encounter consumed with a desire to do everything the King had asked her to do, hungering for more time alone with him. In the following days, she read the letter as a love letter with new understanding and joy, writing down specific messages highlighted for her each day. Pure Heart began to live his life through her and the romance she once felt for him became great love for him. Pure Heart and the King were really one!

Together, Pure Heart and Gloria created a new community. It is written that someday, no one knows the day, Gloria's name will be changed to Glorious! She will be glorious and pure without and within. All who belong to them will live "happily ever after!"

CHAPTER 1

THE INVITATION

The desire to meet with a Holy God is not our idea. In God's love letter, the Bible, He shares with creation His heart's desire that we draw near to Him often. He ~~has~~ tells us of special blessings He bestows when we seek audience with Him. "How happy is the one You choose and bring near to live in Your courts! We will be satisfied with the goodness of Your house, the holiness of Your temple" (Ps 65:4). God yearns to show us the way to live, "Come, eat my bread, and drink the wine I have mixed. Leave inexperience behind, and you will live; pursue the way of understanding" (Pr 9:5-6). God has called to mankind throughout time, "Come, everyone who is thirsty, come to the waters; and you without money, come, buy, and eat! Come, buy wine and milk without money and without cost! Pay attention and come to me; listen, so that you will live. Seek the LORD while He may be found; call to Him while He is near" (Is 55:1, 3, 6).

We must be prepared for an audience with a Holy God. When we accept His provision of adoption through His Son's death and resurrection, we have unrestricted access to His presence. "Therefore let us approach the throne of grace with boldness, so that we may receive mercy and find grace to help us at the proper time" (Heb 4:16). We can come boldly because we come through His Son, Christ Jesus, "and be found in Him, not having a righteousness of my own from the law, but one that is through faith in Christ – the righteousness from God based on faith" (Phil 3:9).

Jesus explained that He is the "door" and "shepherd", through whom we can become royal sons of God. He said "I am the door. If anyone enters by Me, he will be saved and will come in and go out and find pasture. I am the good shepherd. The good shepherd lays down his life for the sheep" (Jo 10:9, 11). When we trust Christ's righteousness before Holy God, we are indwelt by the Spirit of God, giving us access into His presence. "You, however, are not in the flesh, but in the Spirit, since the Spirit of God lives in you" (Rom 8:9a).

In the same way, Jesus is the door to the Tabernacle, and the Great High Priest who escorts us into the presence of Almighty God. "Therefore since we have a great high priest who has passed through the heavens – Jesus the Son of God – let us hold fast to the confession" (Heb 4:14). God wants us to return to Him, resort to Him, draw life from Him, and rest in Him. "For the Lord God, the Holy One of Israel, has said: you will be delivered by returning and resting; your strength will lie in quiet confidence" (Is 30:15a). He wants us to know Him more! "Stop your fighting – and know that I am God, exalted among the nations, exalted on the earth" (Ps 46:10).

Because God desires our heart, "My son, give me your heart, and let your eyes observe my ways" (Pr 23:26), He waits until we turn to Him, seek His face and no longer trust our deceitful heart and understanding.

We need time to withdraw from our realm and draw close to Him in Spirit and in Truth. Seeking the Lord is initiated by us, made possible by Jesus Christ, facilitated by the Holy Spirit, and culminates when the God of the Universe meets with us, infusing His life into ours. We leave filled with quietness and confidence to face the day.

In his book *He Longs for You to See Him*, Chip Ingram explains what we need to do to see God. He compares seeking God to the spiritual change occurring in salvation. This will require everything in our being, our heart, and our emotions. God promises you will find Him if you seek Him. If you ask, He also promises to give you His Spirit to help you know Him.

I believe each human being has three distinct dimensions: the spirit, the soul and the body. When we accept Christ as our Savior, the Holy Spirit comes into our spirit, and the principle of sin moves to the soul and body. His desire is to control the soul, which includes the mind, will and emotions. The body will come under the influence of the Holy Spirit when the soul submits to Him. Preparation brings our soul to the Lord for cleansing and instruction – an audience with a Holy God. Within the soul, the *will* is important, but is not a controlling factor. *Emotions* are important, but they cannot be trusted to control you. The *mind* is the executive officer of the soul, and we begin our preparation by bringing every thought to the obedience of Christ. "We demolish arguments and every high minded thing that is raised up against the knowledge of God, taking every thought captive to the obedience of Christ" (2 Co 10:4b-5). We cry out with the Psalmist, "Bring joy to Your servant's life, since I set my hope in You, Lord. Teach me Your way, LORD and I will live by Your truth. Give me an undivided mind to fear Your name" (Ps 86:4, 11). This passage implies that as we give the Lord complete reign over our *mind*, He can teach us His way. Then we can exercise our *will* to order our steps in the light of His truth. Consequently, our *emotions* come together to fear God alone. This preparation becomes the means by which we daily allow the Holy Spirit to extend His control from our spirit to our soul. "For the word of God is living and effective and sharper than any two-edged sword, penetrating as far as to divide soul, spirit, joints, and marrow; it is the judge of the ideas and thoughts of the heart" (Heb 4:12). Reading God's Word should follow the heart preparation, in order to allow Him access to our mind. He will infuse His mind and his very life into ours, so that we may be His agents in the physical world.

I have practiced this preparation for an audience with Holy God based on the pattern of the Old Testament wilderness Tabernacle for several years. This is not a formula, nor a ritual required in order to be close to God. However, this process is a way I have found useful to prepare my heart as I enter into my daily time with Him. Allowing Jesus to lead me into the throne room, I am prepared to hear God's voice, I renew my appreciation of Him for all He has done in my behalf. Preparation can be quick or drawn out, according to the time I set aside. This always culminates in my recording what I sense God is saying through His Word. The entire process is a prayer.

I begin by preparing my heart to hear from God. Then I read His Word and record His specific wisdom for my life. I conclude by praying for His Spirit to fill and flow through me.

CHAPTER 2

THE APPROACH

We live in a very attractive physical environment. When we begin to prepare our heart for a spiritual encounter, we must purposely draw away from the worldly realm, "God is a spirit, and those who worship Him must worship in spirit and truth" (Jo 4:24). Since we are easily distracted through our human senses, doing this is not easy! Our senses come alive when we purposely approach the "door of the Tabernacle".

On one occasion I could not concentrate on my preparation to meet with God as I heard some very noisy, yapping dogs. Exhausting my efforts to exclude them from my conscious hearing, to no avail, I cried to the Lord to shut the dog's mouths, that I might draw closer to Him. The next thing I knew, I had enjoyed my time with the Lord and the dogs were silent. I knew He had done that for me!

I call this time quieting of the heart. First, we must find a place to be alone. Time must be dedicated to the encounter with God. We need a means of blocking out pressing responsibilities, cares, interruptions, and noises. Other necessary components of preparation are having a Bible, notebook and pen ready to record the exchange. Begin with prayer. Simply *knock* on the door, *seek* His face, and do not forget to *ask* for an audience with Him. Frequently, I must ask for God's help to quiet my heart, and focus my mind on Him alone because often I seem unable to gather up my scattered thoughts and mental entanglements. Jesus is *always* there. He is the door! He stands ready and able to help us as we petition to enter His presence.

One of the functions of the Holy Spirit is leading us into all truth. "When the Spirit of truth comes, He will guide you into all the truth" (Jo 16:13a). I have found that when I read portions from the Old Testament, New Testament, Psalms and Proverbs, during the same quiet time, the Holy Spirit emphasizes truth from at least two, and sometimes all four passages. Repeated truth is not to be dealt with lightly. When God illumines something more than once, He is speaking a specific message to me for that day!

One especially intriguing example I want to share throughout this book is a telescoping of truths from Psalms 19, Psalms 119 and Psalms 115. First, there are six descriptions of God's communication with man. Each one is given an attached benefit (Ps 19:7-9).

1) The LAW of the LORD is PERFECT, converting the soul
2) The TESTIMONY of the LORD is SURE, making wise the simple
3) The STATUTES of the LORD are RIGHT, rejoicing the heart
4) The COMMANDMENT of the LORD is PURE, enlightening the eyes
5) The FEAR of the LORD is CLEAN, enduring forever
6) The JUDGMENTS of the LORD are TRUE and righteous altogether.

God expanded my thinking about each form of communication in Psalms 19 with passages throughout Psalms 119, helping me apply each to one or more of the three dimensions of man: spirit, soul or body.

1) LAW = Instruction about "how to live" – affects the *spirit* and *soul* since the Holy Spirit dwells in the spirit of man, beginning with salvation, and enduring forever. "A person's breath is the lamp of the LORD, searching the innermost parts" (Pr 20:27). "The Spirit is the One who gives life" (Jo 6:63a). Hence, when the soul is converted, the Spirit of God indwells the human spirit.

18

2) TESTIMONIES = God's warnings and witness of Himself – affects the *mind*, since by these the simple are made wise.

3) STATUTES = specific laws God has imposed on mankind – affects the *emotions*, because we're told these rejoice the heart. "When a man's ways please the LORD, He makes even his enemies to be at peace with him" (Pr 16:7).

4) COMMANDMENTS = revelations and charges of God – by these the eye is enlightened, which can affect the *mind*, then the *will*. When we see God and accept his calling for a specific task, our will surrenders to His will.

5) FEAR OF THE LORD = awe and respect for the power and person of a triune God – this affects the *spirit* of man, since it is clean and endures forever.

6) JUDGEMENTS = God's decisions – affect our *spirit, soul* and *body*, and are always right and perfectly just.

Further comparison of truths from Psalms 19 and 119 with the objects in the Tabernacle revealed a possible connection between God's communication to man, the three dimensions of man and the preparation of the heart using the pattern of the tabernacle.

Altar of Burnt Sacrifice – applies to the LAW – spirit and soul

Brass Laver – applies to the TESTIMONIES – mind

Golden Candlestick – applies to the COMMANDMENTS – mind and will

Table of Showbread – applies to the STATUTES - emotions

Altar of Incense – applies to the FEAR OF THE LORD – spirit

Mercy Seat – applies to the JUDGEMENTS – spirit, soul and body

CHAPTER 3

THE ALTAR OF BURNT SACRIFICE

At the door of the Tabernacle, the priest would accept a proper sacrifice to be placed on the bronze altar. The Hebrew word for altar (*mizbeach*) literally means "slaughter place." Sacrifice is essential to relating to God because of our sin. "According to the law almost everything is purified with blood, and without the shedding of blood there is no forgiveness" (Heb 9:22).

Two types of offerings, atonement and consecration, were made at the bronze altar of sacrifice. In I Corinthians 2, Paul wrote of the sacrificial death of Christ, which made a final atonement for our sins. The second type of offering was for consecration. As Christians, we are called to present ourselves as a living sacrifice. "Therefore brothers, by the mercies of God, I urge you to present your bodies as a living sacrifice, holy and pleasing to God; this is your spiritual worship. Do not be conformed to this age, but be transformed by the renewing of your mind, so that you may discern what is the good, pleasing and perfect will of God" (Rom 12:1-2). The purpose of this offering is to continually maintain and readjust our consecration to the Lord.

Before entering into an encounter with a Holy God, we must present to Jesus, our Great High Priest, those things standing in the way of full fellowship with God. "But your iniquities have built barriers between you and your God, and your sins have made Him hide His face from you so that He does not listen" (Is 59:1-2). Jesus paid our sin debt as far as atonement goes. However, we face issues daily which consume our energy, defeat our spirit, cause us to trust ourselves, and drag us into fear and despair.

As these issues are surrendered to Jesus to be placed on the altar of sacrifice, we yield our heart to His control. Things surrendered might include:

Whatever is not of faith (whatever is causing my heart to fear)

Whatever is precious (things I love and desire to come to pass, consuming my energy without the assurance of God's will)

Whatever is heavy (relationships in conflict, problems that burden my heart)

Whatever is perplexing (ideas too complex for me to work out, questions I have no answer for, arguments that have no solution)

"But the one who boasts should boast in this, that he understands and knows Me – that I am the LORD, showing faithful love, justice, and righteousness on the earth, for I delight in these things. This is the Lord's declaration" (Jer 9:24).

During the time spent at the bronze altar of sacrifice, I visualize placing a certain thing into Jesus' hands, watching Him place it on the altar of sacrifice. The flames of fire begin to envelope the item, and I watch the impurities being burned. Whatever remains is purified and can be used with His blessing, for His glory. "You do not want a sacrifice, or I would give it; You are not pleased with a burnt offering. The sacrifice pleasing to God is a broken spirit. God, You will not despise a broken and humbled heart" (Ps 51:16-17).

Fire does not change whether it warms, illumines or burns. When Jesus hands something back, still warm to the touch, I commit it to Him. "Commit your activities to the LORD and your plans will be achieved" (Pr 16:3). If the Holy Spirit illumines my offering I understand more about Jesus and His will in it. "Now we have not received the spirit of the world, but the Spirit who is from God, in order to know what has been freely given to us by God" (I Co 2:12). If God consumes the offering I am free to serve Him unhindered by it. "For the LORD your God is a consuming fire, a jealous God" (Deut 4:24).

Joni EarecksonTada says in *Diamonds in the Dust*, that whatever you give unreservedly to God, He will take. Whatever God takes, He will cleanse. What He cleanses, He fills, and what He fills, He will always use. God will always take what we give Him – when we give to Him without strings attached. If you offer to Him a special friend, He will set about the business of purifying that relationship and filling it with His power and purpose. If you offer God your thought life, He will take that as well, helping you to cleanse your mind and fill it with thoughts that are noble and praiseworthy.

Finally, there are things in my heart that I either cannot or will not see. When I cannot think of anything to give, I simply ask Him to reveal anything that would hinder my time with God. He is always faithful to point out those things that are not pleasing to Him. "All the ways of man seem right to him, but the LORD evaluates the motives"   (Pr 21:2).

By way of example, the International Mission Board of the Southern Baptist Convention shares the story of a church in Tamil Nadu, India which is on the coast with nothing between it and the ocean but flat, desolate land. The pastor of this church felt led to start an orphanage and desired to buy the land between the church and the ocean on which to build it. The landowner, not being a follower of Jesus, refused to sell the land. Seemingly out of spite, she built a wall around the land that came right up to the church. Weeks before the tsunami of December 26, 2004, the pastor was praying asking God why He allowed the landowner to build the wall. Sunday morning, while the church was having its regular Sunday service, the tsunami came ashore. Members were warned minutes before the wave hit and sought refuge on the roof of the church. The wall, built out of spite, acted as a buffer, protecting the church from the waves. The wall was destroyed, but the church was not harmed. The barrier was a blessing of God.

God knows what we can never know. We need to allow Him to have His way in our lives, surrender to His Lordship, and die to our selfish plans and desires. That is what the altar of burnt sacrifice is all about.

CHAPTER 4

THE BRASS LAVER

Immediately after surrendering anything that would not be pleasing to God, I turn to the brass laver. The Old Testament Tabernacle laver was made of bronze and mirrors.

This is a place for confession and cleansing of sin by the Lord.

Titus 3:5 teaches that we are saved by the "washing of regeneration" by the Holy Spirit. In John 13:10 we see that once a person has bathed (is saved), he or she only needs to maintain cleanliness. According to Exodus 30:20-21, priests bathed their entire bodies only once, but maintained cleanliness every time they approached God. Jesus washed the disciples' feet and thereby taught us to keep sin confessed in order to maintain cleanliness as we draw near to God.

When I become pre-occupied with God's glory, I begin to see the sin in my heart. His Word is my mirror to reveal sin. "Search me, God and know my heart; test me and know my concerns. See if there is any offensive way in me; lead me in the everlasting way" (Ps 139:23-24). The Word of God is Jesus Himself: "He wore a robe stained with blood, and His name is called the Word of God" (Rev 19:13). He is standing ready to wash me in preparation for my audience with Holy God. "If we confess our sins, He is faithful and righteous to forgive us our sins and to cleanse us from all unrighteousness" (I Jo 1:9). Confession means agreeing with God about our sin, and we should also agree with Him emotionally about the grief of our sinfulness. After confessing things

I'm aware of, I allow Jesus to show me things I have not seen. "Who perceives his unintentional sins? Cleanse me from my hidden faults" (Ps 19:12). I trust Him to keep His promise.

CHAPTER 5

THE GOLDEN CANDLESTICK

Unburdened and clean, I now enter through the curtain which separates the outer court from "the Holy Place". It is dark except for the light coming from a golden candlestick just inside the curtain. Still escorted by Jesus Christ, my Great High Priest, I realize this is a place of humbling. Here I am made aware of the inadequacy of my understanding. Any truth to be obtained will be given in response to my request for the Holy Spirit to illumine my mind and heart so that I may see what He would have me see as I read His Word. The Holy Spirit residing in my spirit reveals specific truth from His Word, and applies it to my need for the day.

Gazing on the golden candlestick, with its seven lamp bowls and lights, my eyes begin to focus. I see that Jesus is the light! He said "I am the light of the world. Anyone who follows Me will never walk in the darkness but will have the light of life" (Jo 8:12). In the great messianic prophecy of Isaiah, Jesus was described with certain qualities including wisdom, understanding, counsel, might, knowledge, and fear of the Lord God (Is 11:1-2). These same qualities were found in an earlier inspired description of Jesus in Proverbs 8:12-15. Jesus said "The Spirit of the Lord is on Me" (Lu 4:18a) and His being the center stem of the candlestick, embodies all seven of the lights. He wants us to walk in Him and in His knowledge, understanding, counsel, might, wisdom, and fear. We can know things God gives us to know. "For God, who said – light shall shine out of darkness – He has shone in our hearts to give the light of the knowledge of God's glory in the face of Jesus Christ" (2 Co 4:6). Lacking ability to comprehend God with our mind is always humbling. At this place, I must ask for His light of understanding.

Joni EarecksonTada writes in *Diamonds in the Dust* that a person studying Scripture can fail to know the One to whom Scripture was pointing! She encourages us to always ask the Spirit of God to illumine the Word. Otherwise, the study could end up a dry, intellectual exercise. God's Spirit is the one who makes Jesus, the Truth, come alive through the truth of the Word. Even Jesus Himself underscored this in John 16:13-14: "But when he, the Spirit of truth is come, he will guide you into all truth for He shall not speak of himself, but whatsoever he shall hear, that shall he speak, and he will show you things to come. He shall glorify me: for he shall receive of mine and shall show it unto you."

CHAPTER 6

THE TABLE OF SHOWBREAD

Directly across from the candlestick is the Table of Showbread which is a place of thankfulness. Holding twelve loaves of fresh bread each day is a table with great significance, including God's provision and desire for fellowship with His people. In the wilderness wanderings God had a purpose for the trials and provisions of the journey. "He humbled you by letting you go hungry; then He gave you manna to eat, which you and your fathers had not known, so that you might learn that man does not live on bread alone but on every word that comes from the mouth of the Lord" (Deut 8:3). Many years after that time, Jesus said "I assure you: Moses didn't give you the bread from heaven, but my father gives you the real bread from heaven, for the bread of God is the One who comes down from heaven and gives life to the world. I am the bread of life" (Jo 6:32, 35b). He was saying that God caused His chosen people to hunger in order to teach them He was the only thing that could satisfy. This was a truth Jesus used when He was tempted by the evil one. To hunger is to be human, but to hunger for God is to feed on Him. Hunger and thirst after His righteousness and feed on Him in your heart. Taste and see that the Lord is good; it is He who will fill you to satisfaction.

At this point in the preparation of my heart, I begin thanking the Lord for all the things He is for me, has done for me, and will do for me. My heart overflows with thanks as I see how much more He wants to be through me. He creates my hunger so He can reveal His provision, showing me another aspect of His marvelous person. We are nearing the Holy of Holies. Scripture admonishes us to "enter His gates with thanksgiving and His courts with praise. Give thanks to Him and praise His name" (Ps 100:4). My thanks to Him evokes more thanks and it is difficult to move to the next place. It is the place of praise, which is similar to thanksgiving, but excludes everything except God.

CHAPTER 7

THE ALTAR OF INCENSE

Another altar stands in front of the next curtain, the one enclosing the Ark of the Covenant and the Mercy Seat. Incense of the purest kind burns on this altar, the fire having been brought from the Altar of burnt sacrifice. The intensely sweet aroma of the burning incense signifies praise to God from a purified heart. "Whoever sacrifices a thank offering honors Me" (Ps 50:23a) and "You are holy; enthroned on the praises of Israel" (Ps 22:3). Ruth Meyers has written in her devotional book *31 days of Praise* that the word praise means that we admire God for who He is and what He does. Praise can be quiet and meditative. It can also include celebration and exultation for the Lord's majesty and splendor, sovereignty, limitless power, and undeserved love. Praise extols our wonderful God as we exalt and magnify Him, speaking highly to Him and of Him.

Praise is differentiated from thanksgiving in that it is unconditional. Never is it meant as an attempt to influence God to do our bidding. It focuses entirely on him and must be from a pure heart, just as the incense was pure. Efforts of pure praise and adoration have to be cultivated and aided at first. The Psalms give us words to pray back to God. Other helps, such as devotional books or songs, are also valuable when learning to focus on God and His attributes. One motivation to learn and practice prayers of praise is that God delights in it! "The prayer of the upright is His delight" (Pro 15:8b).

CHAPTER 8

THE MERCY SEAT

This place called the Holy of Holies was separated from the rest of the Tabernacle by a thick veil. Previously, once a year, the High Priest would pass beyond this veil to offer sacrifices of atonement for himself and all the people of Israel. Inside the veil was the Ark of the Covenant, which held several objects reminding the people of God's perfection and power. On top of the Ark was the pure gold Mercy Seat covered with the wings of two angels. This is a picture of how Jesus, our Great High Priest took His blood and sprinkled it for a once-for-all atonement for our sins. Now, He eternally intercedes for those who have placed their faith and trust in His sacrifice for their own sins.

My heart is now prepared to encounter a Holy God! I have no need for an earthly priest to enter in for me. Jesus made the final and perfect sacrifice for my sin, allowing me to proceed into the throne room of God Almighty. I enter in only by the presence and authority of Jesus Christ. When I come with a heart prepared to encounter God, I am ready to do three things. *First*, I read His Word, expecting His Spirit to illumine my mind to "see" the things I need. I read the Word systematically, and in four different places (Psalms, Proverbs, Old Testament and New Testament) since Jesus is the living Word and can speak to me from all of His inspired Word. The Apostle Paul prayed for us. "I pray that He may grant you, according to the riches of His glory, to be strengthened with power through His Spirit in the inner man, and that the Messiah may dwell in your hearts through faith. I pray that you, being rooted and firmly established in love, may be able to comprehend with all the saints what is the length and width, height and depth of God's love, and to know the Messiah's love that surpasses knowledge, so you may be filled with all the fullness of God" (Eph 3:16-19). I believe this is what happens in the presence of a Holy God. He infuses His very life, with all of its grace and glory, and His love, for me and others, into and through my very being. Here I am changed into His likeness, given His mind and blessed with His pure heart. A great saint, Hannah Whitehall Smith, wrote in *The Christian's Secret of a Happy Life* about a union of soul which takes place. Separate interests and paths in life are no longer possible. Things that were lawful before become unlawful. The reserve and distance suitable to mere friendship fades into love. The wishes of one become obligations to the other, that it may be fulfilled.

Second, I begin to intercede for other people. When I receive such love from God, I cannot help but think of others. Andrew Murray said in his book *Mighty is Your Hand* that we may not see God, however, we do see men, women and children. They are given, as gifts of God, in order to exercise, strengthen and develop God's love in us. By other's loving actions as well as offenses, they draw the love of God down from its place in the heavenly realm. As we allow it, this great love is perfected in us. It becomes truth, that God Himself is living and loving others from within us.

I feel compelled to pray for the lost, family members, friends, church members, Christian leaders, missionaries, and government officials. I utilize a variety of tools to remember specific names, including e-mails, church prayer lists, mission agency prayer guides, and my own list of people who don't know Jesus. Oswald Chambers defined intercession in his book *My Utmost for His Highest*. He described it as raising ourselves up to the point of getting the mind of Christ regarding the person for whom we are praying.

Third, I petition God for things I need. I ask for wisdom, health, help, counsel, specific words, resources, patience, peace, joy, freedom in relationships, knowledge, creativity, courage, endurance, a better attitude, and many other things.

I have been in the presence of a living, almighty God. From everlasting to everlasting He is God. He has taken time to tell me how much He loves me. Nothing can come between God's love and me! I can rise to face another day of life with the confidence that He is in me, and I am in Him.

CHAPTER 9

THE RESULT

"But if we walk in the light as He Himself is in the light, we have fellowship with one another, and the blood of Jesus His Son cleanses us from all sin" (I Jo 1:7).

Henry Blackaby has written in *Experiencing God* that because God has loved you, He wants you to love Him as well. You can express your love for Him. You can choose life, listen to His voice, hold fast to Him, believe in His only Son, obey His commands and teachings, and be willing to lay down your life for your Christian brothers and sisters. When you do love God, He promises to respond with His blessings. You and your children will live under His blessings. By trusting in Jesus, you have eternal life. The Father will love you. God will come to make His home with you. He will make you more than a conqueror over all difficulties. You will never be separated from His love. God wants you to love Him with all your being. That is the greatest commandment. Your experiencing God depends on your having this relationship of love. A love relationship with God is more important than any other single factor in your life.

Jesus also loves His bride, the church. "The temple of God"; " the body of Christ"; " the beloved bride"; " the fellowship of the saints"; are all Biblical descriptions for the unique, organic entity known as the church. The fruit of the Spirit is expressed primarily in the body. The gifts of the Spirit are expressed primarily through and for the body. When Jesus ascended, He did not leave this world. His presence is still very visible and very real and can only be experienced in His fullness when believers unite in worship and ministry. The church is not an obligation, but a holy presence. It may look and act unholy, however the Spirit of Jesus inhabits His people. For that reason alone, the church requires utmost respect, sincere devotion, and every ounce of passion. It is not merely a group of people we know, it is a group of people Jesus indwells.

What is accomplished in my secret time with the Lord God is made evident in my obedience to what He has communicated to me. I find that there is also a renewed love for His people – His church. It's easy to forget that His goal on earth is the expansion of His kingdom. Sadly, the church experience is not always a great picture of the pure bride of Christ! But, that does not change the truth that He loves the church, and we must also love it. "Christ loved the church and gave Himself for her, to make her holy, cleansing her in the washing of water by the word. He did this to present the church to Himself in splendor, without spot or wrinkle or any such thing, but holy and blameless" (Eph 5:25b-27). Jesus is in charge of the cleansing and the presenting. He will present her to Himself having been changed from Gloria to Glorious! I am part of that great promise, and everything I do after my encounter with Holy God is part of this mighty work to bring us together as His body on earth, and His bride in the Kingdom.

In scripture, following the second death, where death and hell are cast into the lake of fire, the New Jerusalem, the Holy City, is described. "Then I saw a new heaven and a new earth, for the first heaven and the first earth had passed away and the sea existed no longer. I also saw the Holy City, New Jerusalem, coming down out of heaven from God, prepared like a bride adorned for her husband. Then I heard a loud voice from the throne: Look! God's dwelling is with men, and He will live with them. They will be His people, and God Himself will be with them and be their God" (Rev 21:2b-3). In the very next verse, God said "Behold, the tabernacle of God is with men, and He will dwell with them, and they shall be His people, and God Himself shall be with them, and be their God" (Revelation 21:3). I will be there – part of the glorious bride, the church! It will be a wondrous feeling to move through the heavenly Tabernacle having been glorified in my body and cleansed from every blemish. Praise will not be hard. All need for intercession will have passed away, and I will have perfect communion forever with Holy God. Until then I'll keep meeting with God, receiving His life, and allowing His love to flow through me to others, especially to His bride, the church.

PREPARATION OF THE HEART FOR AN AUDIENCE WITH A HOLY GOD

Approach the Tabernacle	Quiet the Heart
Altar of burnt sacrifice	Throw off weights and hindrances
Brass laver	Confess sin and be cleansed
Golden candlestick	Ask for Holy Spirit illumination
Table of showbread	Be thankful and grateful
Altar of incense	Offer praise and adoration to God
Mercy seat	Listen to God – receive His life
Rise to meet the day	Begin the day ready to obey, filled with God's love, and eager to share His love with others, especially the church!

This is the way I approach Holy God. It can take a few moments, or an hour. I especially love the times in which I am not rushed. Time constraints can be managed so they do not keep me from preparing and entering in with my whole heart. My prayer is that this will be a tool in His hand to lead you into a more meaningful encounter with Him.

ENTER IN!

About the Author

Barbara Garner is a wife, mother of three grown children, and grandmother of five. A graduate of Baylor University, and Texas Woman's University, she has served forty three years in a variety of ministry positions in seven states. She is a teacher and librarian, and currently resides in Alpharetta, Georgia, where here husband, George, is on staff with the North American Mission Board of the Southern Baptist Convention.

Breinigsville, PA USA
02 February 2010
231737BV00001B/7/P